Thrift

Making Massive Money from items at Thrift Store Prices by Selling them for Huge Retail Profits

(Thrifting on Scale, Dominating the Flipping Market Online and off)

Table of Contents

Introduction

First of all, I want to thank you as well as congratulate you for making a great decision of downloading the book, *"Thrift"*.

For most people, creating a business of their own may be quite difficult, especially if you are lacking funds to start up the business. However, Thrifting offers a low barrier to entry business model which is easy to get into, and doesn't require a great deal of cash at all. If you are new to the idea of thrifting, let this book be your guide on how to learn the basics and allow us to teach you some techniques to make the most out of your Thrift Store buying and selling journey. We will provide you a proven framework, and methodology for making it big in this easy to do (and immensely fun) field.

This book contains proven steps and strategies on how to make massive money for your eBay (or other online) store just by selling local Thrift Store product. This book will also give you the advantage that you need to become a successful business owner in this field. It is tough maintaining business through eBay, particularly if you are green to the idea of selling online. Most of the time, customers are always looking for the next big fad or trend. In this light, it would be wise to bring in unique items and products that you can find in Thrift Stores. Thrift Stores are available in any area of the country (including internationally) and they offer a great opportunity to make huge amounts of money from items that people might be looking for elsewhere in the country.

Bottom line: Thrift Store items sell just as well as pricey brand name products almost 100% of the time. Once you come to that realisation and mindset, you will become truly successful in this field and will be running to the local Thrift Store to find that next 'thing' you can sell on your online store; most likely something that you can sell for ten to even one hundred times the original value. All it requires is the right mindset and our proven methodology and framework.

It's time for you to be financially free and live the easy life you deserve and this book is a helpful guide on how to reach your business potential. It will run through many aspects of building a business on eBay using thrift stores and retail shops and give you the tools you need to succeed.

Sit back and enjoy the ride.

Chapter 1: The Fundamentals of Thrifting

With the current state of the economy, it is no longer a wonder why many people go thrifting. Thrift stores offer items, which you may no longer see in most retail shops and big box stores such as vintage items. At other times, you may also see item brands, which are not sold in your area such as international item brands. However, what makes thrifting special is not only credited to the unique finds that a thrift store may offer, but also to the very cheap prices that goes with each item. All you need to do is to develop an expert eye in finding these special goods as well as a quick mind to help you find and purchase the best item that will your budget.

Still not getting the idea behind thrifting?

Thrifting comes in many definitions. Among the famous ones would include thrifting defined as the act of going to thrift stores, second-hand shops, garage sales, vintage stores, flea markets, or even charitable organizations with the intent to shop for goods. Most often than not, people who go thrifting on these shops with the intention of finding unique or rare items at a very cheap price.

At times, thrifting is also defined as the act of recycling pre-owned products or items and finding new use for them. Another definition for thrifting is the practice of restrained spending habits through the purchase of goods and items from very cheap shops as well as owning pre-loved items.

The Other Side of Thrifting

Though thrifting is commonly associated by most people with shopping and owning items, entrepreneurs have given a new face to thrifting. The other side of thrifting is leaned towards earning money rather than spending it. Most entrepreneurs call this as the business of **"Thrift Store Flipping"** or **"Thrift Shop Selling"**. This is not the same as owning a thrift store, renovating it, and then selling it again. That is a different idea. Instead, thrift store flipping allows an entrepreneur to basically purchase unique and special thrift store finds for a cheap price so they can sell it online or offline for higher prices.

Thrift store flipping is a lucrative business in its own right - especially if you can spot and purchase the best items that would appeal to many people. This business is a cheaper way to start your own store. For one reason, you will not need a huge capital to start it. You will also not need to have a physical store built as the option of flipping thrift stores online is always available particularly in websites like eBay.

To make better use of your thrifting skills and earn money at the same time, it is suggested that you try flipping thrift store items.

Chapter 2: Thrift Shop Selling Online is the New Antiquing

As mentioned earlier, thrifting is no longer solely linked to shopping for thrift store items, it is also now linked to selling items from thrift stores. Though this can be done by creating a physical shop to store and sell your goods, the most practical way, especially for beginners, would be to make the most of what the Internet has to offer - a digital avenue. Many have already started this online business, but many are still welcome since thrift stores offer different items in different locations. Therefore, if you want to start your own, it is not yet too late and if you are not yet convinced of the benefits that thrift shop selling can give you, by all means read on so you will not be missing this awesome opportunity.

Benefits of Thrift Shop Selling

Thrift shop selling has tons of benefits that a thrift shop flipper can enjoy. Here are some of them:

Unique Finds = Unique Items to Sell

Thrift stores carry different items. Some may not really be good or of high quality yet, it cannot be discounted that the possibility of getting unique finds and rare items is present. There are even thrift stores, which are classified as high end since they are located on the high-end parts of the town and because they carry high-end pre-loved items. In that essence, as soon as you spot and purchase a good find, you can re-sell it on your online store for a higher price. This will make your store unique.

Cheap thrift store prices offer the possibility of higher earnings for you.

Thrift stores are not called as such for nothing. The major reason they are called thrift stores is because they carry different products for very cheap prices. Taking this into consideration, the items that you choose will most likely have lower prices compared to most major retail and big box stores.

Avoid the hassle of finding several wholesale suppliers.

Usually, you will need to list and contact different suppliers just so you can fill your store with items to sell. However, if you go thrift shopping, all you need to do is list the best thrift stores offering unique goods and cheap prices. Remember, thrift stores carry different items. Though some may cater more on garments, there are also many thrift stores offering a wide array of goods. So, be sure to list and check those every time you go thrift shopping for your store.

Avoid renting or owning huge warehouses to store your goods.

Normally, if you are to build a brick and mortar business leaned on selling goods, you will need to also rent or own huge warehouses so you will be able to store your goods and keep your stocks. If you start thrift selling instead, your basement can double as a warehouse for storing the goods.

Moreover, if you are reside near the thrift store, you can just purchase one item, get pictures of it for selling, and then run down the store if people start to order the item. With the latter, you wouldn't even need a storage space.

Chapter 3: Why Thrift Store Items are Best for eBay

There are many ways on how you can sell your thrift store finds. You can create your own website or even just create social networking pages. However, the best site where you can sell your thrift store items would be in eBay. eBay is an online shopping website that caters to millions of shoppers daily. You will find good business in selling your thrift store items here. Here are some of the reasons why thrift store items are best for eBay.

eBay offers different selling options.

Unlike other online shopping sites, eBay offers different selling formats such as auction-style format, "Buy It Now" format, and the eBay shopping cart format. Each format provides different benefits that you can take advantage of.

For instance, **auction-style** is a format where a buyer can bid an item from the starting price placed by the seller. The bidder with the best deal will win the item when the listing ends. *This format is best-suited for thrift store items which are rare, unique, or hard to find. You can place these items for bidding so you can get the best price for it instead of just putting a fixed amount.*

Another format would be, "**Buy It Now**". This format allows the buyer to purchase the item immediately in a set or fixed price. This is an option that you can also pair with the auction-style format. *You can utilize this format if the thrift* *store items you are selling are not so rare yet have limited stocks.*

The third format is the **eBay shopping cart**. This option is similar to most online shopping sites such as Amazon. With this format, the buyer will be able to shop many items from your online store easily. They can browse everything you have and pick the items that want. They can then purchase all of the items that they picked in just one transaction. If you offer "Buy It Now" items in your store, buyers can also add them in their shopping cart by simply clicking on the "Add to cart" button. What's more is that, the buyer can also purchase from other sellers in the same transaction as long as the sellers accept PayPal payment. *This format is best if you are selling thrift store items which are not rare or those which are not limited in stock. For example, if you have a thrift store supplier who agreed to supply you or restock your inventory for Item A in a regular basis, you can utilize this selling option.*

eBay offers a global marketplace for your thrift store goods.

For quite some time now, eBay has been used by people from all over the world to sell their products and goods. If you will be using eBay to sell your unique thrift store goods, you will open an online store for all of the world to see. There is definitely someone out there is happy to purchase the goods that you are selling. Moreover, eBay has developed a Global Shipping Program so that you can easily ship your items to international buyers.

eBay provides an excellent Search Engine Optimization system.

Search Engine Optimization or SEO is a system that ranks specific items or products in the search results. This way, when a buyer searches for a specific item, the search engine can produce and rank results that are best suited for the search executed by the buyer. This is a good opportunity for you as you can take advantage of this eBay feature. If you optimize your products well using keywords and SEO-friendly descriptions, you will be able to land a good place in eBay's search results.

Chapter 4: Finding the Best Items to Thrift

As a seller, it is very important that you take your time in researching the best thrift store items to purchase. Investing extra time will help ensure that you will be able to get better earnings and faster sales transaction in your eBay online store. To begin a lucrative eBay business, you will need to research certain aspects of your inventory. Here is a short guide that will aid you in finding the best items to thrift and re-sell in your store.

Hot Items

Though hot items may seem profitable, you will have to consider that you are selling thrift store items. This means, that if iPods are the craze on eBay and you find a pre-loved iPod in a thrift store or garage sale, you may have difficulty selling the item despite the craze. Many buyers would like to purchase hot items which are brand new and those that have warranties or guarantees. If you are selling pre-loved thrift store items falling in this category, it may take a while before the hot item to sell. More so, hot items are being sold by many sellers already so you may either end up with the item for a long time or not be able to sell it at all.

Typical Retail Items

Typical retail items have a 50-50 chance of selling well on eBay since these items may be found in major retail stores. If you found such items on thrift stores, you may need to consider a few factors before purchasing them for flipping purposes.

One factor that you need to consider is the **price**. Is it cheaper than the ones in the retail stores? If it is, compute how much you will be profiting from re-selling it and consider if the re-sell price (your profit included) is still cheaper than the ones from retail stores.

Consider the **authenticity** or **quality** of the item. Is the item original? Is the item high quality? Is there any damage or factory defect on it? If your answer to those questions is a resounding "No!", then don't purchase the items as these will just affect your credibility and rating as an eBay seller.

So, when can you sell typical retail items? You can sell such items if you found designs or variations which are not found in retail stores as these can be considered collectible. You can also sell typical retail items if they are not available in the local shops where your target market are located. For example, you are targeting a state in the US and you found great retail items from an Asian thrift store. If you feel that the possibility of those items to exist in your target state is low, you can then purchase those goods for your store.

Unique or Hard to Find Items

Remember, thrift shop selling is not only limited to thrift stores, you can also purchase goods from garage sales, flea markets, specialized thrift stores, and more. In this light, it would be practical for you to purchase items which are unique and hard to find yet still have the ability to sell. For instance, if you go to high-end thrift stores, you may just find in the racks branded pre-loved or slightly used garments and accessories. Usually, these will be cheaper than the ones found in retail stores and the quality may not be as bad. In some occasions, you may even find branded pre-loved items, which are no longer in the circulation yet still marketable. You will just need to do some research on such.

Antique Items

Some items being sold many thrift stores, garage sales, and flea markets may also pass as antique items. Such items are still marketable especially if they are still in good or working quality. You can have these items put up for auction on eBay to get a better price instead of just tagging them fixed prices.

***

Tips in Purchasing Your Chosen Items from Thrift Stores

Those prices from thrift stores often come very cheap, you can still slash a small fraction of the price without low-balling the thrift store owner and still get the best items that you want to purchase. here are some tips that you can implement.

Negotiate But Not to the Point of Haggling Too Much

Needing to spend a dollar or two less on that bookshelf? Contingent upon the store that you are visiting, it is sensible to make a somewhat lower offer. Individuals like to be paid forthright, so simply remember that. There is always room to barter when you are walking through a resale or thrift shop. These prices are considered to be base prices.

Before you try to negotiate, you must first think of a price that you are willing to pay for the item. This price should be the most you would pay for it. Just as you have the maximum price you would pay for the item, the shop has a minimum price they are willing to take. The act of negotiating is where the two people come to a fair compromise in between the prices that both have in mind for the transaction.

Do Not Limit Yourself

Keep in mind that just because the item is not something you would necessarily own does not mean that someone else with a different style would not want the item. It's a decent thought to purchase items from a mixture of classes such as garments, furniture, memorabilia, machines, apparatuses, and so on.

In any case, it is not suggest simply obtaining the same number of arbitrary things that you can discover while at the thrift store. Get educated into "Thrift" history and make some sense over what individuals are searching for while on the web.

Take books, for instance. Individuals are continually searching for them, correct? Students, graduates, libraries, and book lovers, to name a few, are continually searching for something new to read. You can purchase books for low prices at most thrift stores and it's superbly sensible to offer them at a somewhat higher cost on eBay. You did the diligent work of discovering this stuff, yes? So, you deserve a piece of the pie.

Go For the Discounts

A few thrift stores offer exceptional rebates depending upon the day. As such, some thrift stores may indicate their rebates, sales, and discounts with the use of a labeling system like yellow or red tags placed on some items. However, without a doubt, chances are that you will sometimes discover garments that you totally must purchase, reduced or not. An example for such store would be Goodwill. There are many Goodwill branches located all over the states. With this in mind, you will have an easy access to your inventory. This also means that you will be able to get items cheaply, sell them at fair prices, and even deliver in a timely manner.

Most thrift stores and resale shops have certain days when they run their sale promotions on specific types of items. For example, on Mondays the thrift store may take an extra 25% off yellow-tagged items. These thrift stores normally have a digital flyer that you can have delivered to your email to keep track of what days they have sale promos.

Find Thrift Stores in Well-To-Do Areas

It is best to visit thrift stores that are located in busy and more expensive areas. One might even say "ritzy" areas. These areas are those, which have the property values that are double the typical property value. What this means to you is that those in this area "have money". These people drop the items off at the local thrift store to be sold to those looking for these items that are gently used.

You are more likely to find items that are name brand, more expensive, and like new. This will open up a larger profit margin than a used sweater that is dated. Taking advantage of the inventory in these areas will give you a wider selection in price differences and offer you a wider range of customers. Thus, building up a better customer base.

Chapter 5: The Key to "Marketing" Products on eBay

Having great products to sell on eBay is not the sole thing that will help you earn money. These great thrift store items will just go to waste if no one knows your store is even existing. In this case, the best thing you can do to attract buyers to your eBay store is by marketing them.

The key to marketing products on eBay is by **utilizing the different marketing tools available on the site as well as additional online marketing strategies**. If you are a new eBay seller, marketing your products may take a bit of your time since you are still introducing your store to the pool of buyers surfing and browsing for products on eBay.

eBay Marketing Tools

eBay has a set of marketing tools that you can use to market your products. You can utilize these marketing tools so as to attract more customers to your eBay online store.

One marketing tool offered by eBay is the **Cross-Promotion system**. This system can be activated so your products can be cross promoted in the different parts of eBay. If your products are promoted in the website, more buyers will stumble upon your products.

Another eBay marketing tool that you can use would be the **Promote Similar Listings** option. This option will allow possible exposure of your products on other seller's listings as long as you have similar products. So, if a specific seller has regular buyers and you appear on their listing page, that seller's buyers may take notice of what you are selling and check you out.

Promote Your Other Products to Your Buyers

This may sound silly, but you can actually promote your store and your products to your own buyers. For example, if you will be deliver items to your buyers, you can include delivery stickers, postcards, business cards, and what-nots on the parcel. Such items should include your seller contact information such as your website address, if you have any, or your eBay store link so the buyers will better remember you. This simple act of promotion can bring repeat customers to you and if your customers were pleased of the professionalism you showed by including such promotional items in their parcel, they may even promote you personally to their friends or even pass to their friends the business card that you sent.

Marketing Through Your Product Descriptions

In your item descriptions, you can include texts such as "Check out my other products here" or "My other auctions are found here" Make sure the statement is clickable or is linked to your listings so that the customers can just easily click it and check out what else you have to offer. In addition, ensure that the statement is bold, large, and bright so, it can attract the attention of the buyer.

Promote Your Products on Other Sites

It is unwise to just set up your eBay store and completely forget about it. You must do all the promoting that you can for people to know that your eBay store exists. You can do this by promoting your products on other sites such as Facebook (through a Facebook Page), blogs, and your own site so that search engines can index your eBay store and lead traffic to your storefront.

Email Marketing Can Also Help

If you can get email lists of customers, you can also do email promotions so you can inform buyers about discounts and promos that you have. You can also use this to promote new thrift store finds that you have acquired.

Chapter 6: Creating Urgency and Scarcity in Your Products

Getting customers gobbling up your items can be a battle. This can bring about a long, drawn out deal process with customers considering purchasing from your store for a considerable length of time, weeks, or months. You will need to pay attention to the thrift items that sell. Luckily, there are ways to introduce your inventory and create a sense of urgency to purchase the items.

What is Scarcity?

If you have a thrift item that you would like to sell that is considered **unique or rare**, it is best to make sure that **you have it listed as such in the description**. This will show them that thrift this item will be sold decently fast and that if they do not purchase it soon they will lose their chance.

Another way to create scarcity is to **only list one or two of the same item** that is in demand. If you have 20 to 50 of the item listed, then the customer will think they have time to shop around on other store sites. Should you list that you only have a few of these items, you will be able to sell them much faster. The customer will be afraid to lose out on the deal that you have set in front of them.

Show customers your stock numbers. A standout amongst the most widely recognized techniques is to place the quantity of stock that your store has left on the item page for clients to see. This will trigger earnestness to clients, as they will see that there are just a couple of items left until the chance to purchase is gone.

Tell customers you are low in stock. Having stock numbers listed will tell clients that that specific product is low in stock. It's a basic thing. However, it is powerful, as clients will feel the need to promptly purchase before the item vanishes. ASOS expertly tells their clients by showing on the item page when an item is low in stock.

Make it Limited Time Only

Shortage does not need to be particularly identified with the stock, as utilizing offers, advancements, and arrangements are also possible. Putting a set date for an offer to lapse can be an extraordinary allure for clients to start a purchase. This will show that they only have a limited time to purchase the item and listing the quantity of the items in stock is less relevant to the purchase urgency.

Make it Seasonal

This is a great idea for inventory that fits in certain areas of the year, whether it is items for summer or items for a holiday. When selling item for seasonal and promotional purposes, it is best to ensure that you have that detail listed in the product descriptions. Begin selling the seasonal items at least a month before the season so those who are looking can purchase from your store earlier. Keep the items listed during the season as well. Put a deadline date on the seasonal items so customers know when they are able to purchase and when they can no longer purchase the items you have for sale for the specific season.

Chapter 7: Taking Your Business to the Next Level

If you have already established your eBay online storefront and you have mastered the arts of promoting to attract more buyers, it is now time for you to start taking your business to the next level. You would not want to stay at your current selling status as you will want to earn more from selling thrift store items on eBay. If you are to consider taking your business to the next level, it would be best to have a business plan so you will be right on track to scaling up the thrift store flipping business.

7 Steps in Writing a Business Plan

A business plan in front of your face will help you in developing your business idea better as well as keep you walking on the right path to success. Formulate your business plan by following these steps.

Step 1: Business Upscaling Purpose

With upscaling your business in mind, you need to write a purpose for doing so. This does not need to be long, as a sentence for this will do. Just make sure that your statement is concise and reasonable.

Step 2: Define the Problem/s

You have to outline possible problems that you are encountering at the moment. Also include in this step the current solutions that you are using. For example, you can list that you are having tough time in entertaining all the sales that come in your eBay online store since you are operating the store on your own. Then, just for the purpose of this example, you can list that the solution you are currently using is by taking extra time to work on the orders from your large number of buyers.

Step 3: Propose Possible Solutions

In this step, you have to propose or list down possible solutions to the problems stated in Step 2. For the problem stated above, you can list a couple of solutions such as hiring someone to help you out in managing the business or outsourcing the job to a virtual assistant. You may also list out the pros and cons for each so you can better weigh your options.

Step 4: Define Your Current Market Size

Defining your current market size will help you in determining whether you will be able to manage the business upscale that you desire or if you are capable of implementing the solutions that you have proposed.

Step 5: Re-define Your Product Line Up

Since you will be upscaling the business, you might as well re-define the product line up that you currently have. Will you be adding other products? Will you be increasing the amount of inventory or stock for each product? Up to how much should you increase based on your current market size? Will your current budget or capital allow this? You should ask these questions so you can gauge the possibility of updating the product line up.

Step 6: Simple Sales and Expense Forecast

This does not have to be exact at this time. It is more of an estimate of what is to be spent and what is to be made during the course of one year when your business is supposed to upscale. It is a rule of thumb that if you should purchase items from a thrift store, you will be selling it for double of what you paid for it.

You will need to make an **estimated expense list**. Keep in mind that it is better to overestimate than to underestimate in order to ensure that you have enough capital to begin with. For the expense list, you will need to add in all of the materials that you will need in order to operate. This includes a printer for receipts to send with the items, ink and paper for the printer, binders and a filing cabinet to keep track of all transactions and financial information for tax purposes, shipping supplies, and other items for operations. This will also include a budget to obtain the upscaled inventory. The upscaled inventory budget is what you will use to purchase items from the thrift stores.

Once you have your expense list made, you will need to build a **cash flow forecast**. This is where the expenses that you have spent are listed to see where this leaves you as far as profit is concerned. For example, if you have an expense list that includes $500 for supplies and $1000 for your inventory, then your total expense list will cost $1,500. Using the rule of thumb, which was previously stated about selling the inventory for double of what you purchased it for, you will then be able to deduce that you need to resale the inventory for $2,000. Therefore, you will have a profit of $500 within the first year. Come next year, the profit will be even larger since you will no longer need to purchase equipment like printers or filing cabinets.

Step 7: Scheduling Tasks and Reviewing the Schedule

This step is crucial especially if you want to take your business to the next level. Scheduling tasks and assigning specific responsibilities to those who are involved should you have employees is necessary. You will need to manage those under you as well as the tasks that you set forth for yourself and others. Keep a scheduler. This can be on your computer or you can go the paper route and use a planner. (The planner should be included in the expense list.)

Being accountable for your business is the key when you are deciding to be a business owner. This means that, you will need to review all of the information that deals with the business. You will need to ensure that you review the schedule for shipping, selling, inventory control, and other aspects that need your attention during specific times. You will also need to review your plan and update, as needed, any information that deals with running of your business.

Step 8: Executive Summary

This is where sum up everything that you have set forth for a plan. It is to help you focus on your goals, as well as present to others what you may want to "bring on board".

Step 9: Print the Plan

You will need to print the business plan so that you can have it in front of you all the time. This is done for multiple reasons. It will keep you focused on your goals and allow you to stay on track. Another reason is so that you can make notes as you alter your plan and can change it on the copy later, then reprint if you need to.

***

Improved Cash Flow through Overhead Expense Reduction and Improved Efficiency

Aside from creating a business plan you will also need to take time in planning to improve your cash flow since you will be upscaling the business. Two major factors that can greatly improve cash flow includes overhead expense reduction or operating expense reduction and efficiency improvement.

Reduce Overhead Expense

Overhead expense or operating cost are ongoing expenses to keep the business operational. Such expenses are important, but can be trimmed down or reduced so as to increase the business' cash flow. Overhead thrift store flipping may include, but are not limited to advertising fees, rent (if you are renting a different basement space for storage), repairs (for the computer you are using), supplies, telephone bills, taxes, travel expenses, and utilities.

Some of these overhead costs may not be easily reduced like taxes, but you can definitely workout something with the others. For instance, you can reduce advertising fees, but doing manual advertisement instead of hiring professional advertisers to promote or advertise your business. If your target market include college students, you can hire a person on Fiverr.com to pass out flyers for you for just $5. Still on Fiverr.com, you can also hire a person to promote your product to their followers on Twitter, Facebook, and the likes. This is still for $5. Rent reduction can be done if you will be able to maximize the space through proper product organization. This way, you will be able to store more thrift items for the same rental fee. As for supplies, make a checklist of the supplies that you are using. Make sure that you list everything and check the ones which your business can live without. Alternatively, if you really need all the supplies in your list, you can just reduce the amount of the said supplies instead of totally removing them from the list. Travel expenses can also be reduced by planning ahead of time. Schedule the dates when you will need to go out thrifting. Strategically plan which thrift store you will visit first so as to save gas or commute fair. This will also save you energy in the process.

Improved Efficiency

Improved efficiency is also important as this mean more work gets done. Efficiency can be improved by creating a schedule that you will be able to follow well. This schedule must lean towards your most productive hours so that you can ensure your business will be well taken care of. Moreover, you need to make sure that this schedule made in a strategic manner. You can even make it into a form of a checklist so you can check the things that you are getting done. This will improve your motivation better.

On the other hand, you can also try to outsource some of your tasks so you can get more done in the same time span that you usually work. You can train a virtual assistant or a VA from time to time. Outsourcing your job to the right people can help you reduce cost and improve efficiency in the process.

The Pareto Principle or the 80-20 Rule

On top of those factors presented, you also need to deeply root in your personality the 80-20 rule or what is also popularly known as the "Pareto Principle" and the "rule of the vital few."

This rule was developed by a 20th century figure by the name of Joseph Juran. The 80-20 rule explains that 80% of the outcomes can be credited to 20% of the causes for that a specific event. This rule will assist you in identifying issues as well as determining which of the operating factors are most crucial and must receive the most attention based on how efficient this factor is in using resources. In this light, the resources must be given to address the input factor having the most influence on the final results that you are trying to achieve.

In analogy, this can be liken to the idea that 80% of the nation's wealth is managed by only 20% of the populace.

Chapter 8: Scaling Your Thrift Business for the Long Term

In order to scale up your business for the long term, you will need to understand a few key points when dealing with profit margins, inventory, and other aspects of owning a business that runs on inventory. It is important to not only shop for the right pieces to sell, but also to factor in pricing and expenses when offering them online to your customers. This will ensure that your business will not only survive, but also thrive in the future.

Filling the Inventory

Filling your inventory is an important matter that you need to consider if you want to scale up. Scaling up entails a larger inventory so you can cater to more buyers. In this aspect, it would only be wise to check for reliable thrift stores, which can supply goods to you in a regular basis. If you stumble upon these reliable thrift stores, you must list them down and contact them regarding any business proposal that you have. Business proposals are going to be useful in such situation, since you can negotiate for a lower price that is still fair to the thrift store owner. This way, you can build a good partnership with them and still earn sufficient profit.

Prepare a Bigger Capital

At this point, you should have also prepared a bigger capital since you are expanding the business for good. You should take time in doing your accounting or ask assistance from an expert or professional so as to get your numbers right. The budget must be allotted accordingly so your cash flow will be bigger. You do not want to experience budget insufficiency when your Business 2.0 is operating.

Know the Resale Price of Your Target Items Even Before You Buy Them

It is also very important to know what the items sell for as far as the retail price is concerned, even before you purchase them. This can be an exceptionally troublesome assignment in light of the fact that there are truly many brands available. When going thrifting, you need to invest extra time in computing for resale prices even when you are inside the store. This may eat up a chunk of your time, but this will help build your inventory. Moreover, as soon as everything is listed in your records already, you will not need to do resale price computation in the future, unless the prices change.

Learn about Profit Potential in Detail

Since you are already gearing towards a bigger business for the long term, it would be wise to invest some time in learning about profit potential in detail. The profit potential is also called **profit margin**. The profit margin is the "*playing room*" that you have between what the item costs and what amount the item will be sold for. For example, if you purchased an item for $5 and sold it for $10, then the profit margin would be $5. Here is a simple equation to help you figure out the profit margin per item.

Item Selling Price – Item Expense (what you paid for it) = Profit Margin

You also need to take a note of this in a separate notebook so you can refer to them when needed.

Chapter 9: Automating Aspects of Your Thrift Business

After planning for an upscaled business and actually implementing those plans, you will now need to let money work for you by means of taking advantage of the automating aspects of your thrift business. This will make work more efficient and at the same time allow you to earn more. Automation offers increased productivity to your business. Moreover, you will have more free time to work on the other aspects of your business or start a new one altogether - all thanks to automation and your thrift business.

There are different ways, ranging from simple to complex ways, that you can do to incorporate automation in your eBay thrift business.

eBay Automation Tools

Since you will be utilizing eBay for your thrift business, you might as well use the automation tools that they are offering.

One of the automation tools offered by eBay include **Selling Manager Pro**. Selling Manager Pro is a paid tool. This tool allows you to auto list or re-list your products as well as allow you to set preferences in terms of sending automatic emails and positive feedback. It also allows you to manage your inventory, make use of extra options for automated product listing and re-listing, as well as provide monthly sales reports.

Selling Manager, on the other hand, is a free version. This version allows you to manage and create your listings, track status of sales, and perform post-sales activities like printing shipping labels or leaving feedback.

Another eBay automation tool that you can use is the **Turbo Lister**. This tool is free of charge. It allows you to have the ability to edit or upload items in bulk. It also aids you in creating listings that look professional. It even has a search tool to help you in finding items quickly. On top of that, it also offers special views so you can have better control over your listings . Saving listing templates can be done with Turbo Lister as well.

File Exchange is also an automation tool offered by eBay. This is also a free tool that allows you to list multiple items using just a single file. You can list items by means of using flat files from an MS Excel Spreadsheet, MS Access, as well as other inventory software applications.

Outsourcing of Work

Aside from utilizing eBay automation tools, you can also automate your business by means of outsourcing work or hiring employees to do a specific task in your behalf. Outsourcing jobs to other people will not only help you in saving time, but also save money in the process. If you outsource a specific job, you will earn extra time to other money-generating businesses or even use that time for relaxation or a long-awaited vacation. Moreover, when you outsource tasks, you will have access to a pool of expert people who are already very good at doing specific jobs. Moreover, if you will be outsourcing work online, you will not need to shell out extra cash for some overhead cost since your online employee handles those. That is efficiency and overhead cost reduction right off the bat.

Automating Social Media Tasks for Marketing

Marketing is still very important to help your business grow and social media is a great partner to boost your marketing to the next level. Guess what? Even such tasks can be automated.

Facebook is a good avenue to market your thrift business as more people are getting active on Facebook. In Facebook, you can be more efficient by automating your posts on your Facebook Page. ***Schedule posts ahead of time***. This is extremely useful when you are posting promotional offers, discounts, and seasonal items. You can also ***connect your blog feed to Facebook*** so that your blog posts are automatically posted on your Facebook page. ***Make use of the analytics*** to check what people on Facebook are checking on your page.

Zapier is another automating tool that you can use to automate different tasks between online services. How does this work? Say, you have a new video, which you have uploaded on your own YouTube channel, if you set Zapier to send out a tweet every time you upload a video, it will do just that. The good thing about Zapier is you can set up multiple "zaps" for different services. Zapier can be used free of charge or you can take advantage of the extra features by subscribing under paid premium plans.

Chapter 10: The Best Online Resources For Thrifting

You are now equipped with tons of great tips and ideas on how to start and even upscale your thrift business on eBay. However, learning is a continuous process. If you want to learn more about thrifting, here are some of the best online resources that you can use for thrifting.

Thrifting Website

Skip McGrath's Online Seller's Resource

http://www.skipmcgrath.com/

This website offers tons of great online selling information especially for eBay entrepreneurs. He has lists for helpful trainings, newsletters, free articles, tools, and resources.

Thrifting for Profit

http://thriftingforprofit.com/

This website offers a wealth of knowledge all about thrifting. The site offers tips and shares experiences through articles and podcasts which are all posted on the site.

Jordan Malik - Honest Online Selling

http://jordanmalik.com/blog/

This website is also dedicated to sharing online selling experiences as well as giving tips on how you can best utilize eBay in selling your thrift items. The book offers resources, reviews, one-on-one help, and many others.

Outsourcing Work

Find, Hire & Train Virtual Assistants To Find Inventory Online While You Sleep (Video Course)

http://thesellingfamily.com/trainings/train-your-va-for-online-sourcing/

It is best to hire employees to help you get the job done, in this light it would be great if you have a VA or a virtual assistant by your side. Don't know how to hire a good VA? You can try undergoing this training so you will know the basics of finding, hiring, and training virtual assistants to help you in your business. Once you have found a good VA to work with, you will be able to get things done - even while you sleep!

Others

You can also make use of these other resources so you can push your thrift item selling business to a bigger scale. You can get tips and strategies on resources such as:

Rob Anderson's The Dollar Moves Youtube Channel (Rob Anderson provides tips on how to earn more and make every dollar work for you. Great for business start ups.)

https://www.youtube.com/user/dollarmoves

Ask Janelle Podcast (An e-commerce pioneer who can answer eBay seller help questions on selling, marketing, and the likes)

http://wsradio.com/?s=ask+janelle

The Dani App (A Facebook group dedicated to helping thrifters, eBay, Amazon, and Etsy sellers get the most out of their business)

http://www.facebook.com/groups/TheDanniApp/

Conclusion

Thank you again for downloading this book!

I hope this book was able to help you organize your business plan and begin selling your way to financial freedom or at the least aid you in paying off your monthly bills with ease.

The next step is to take what you have learned from this book and apply it to your business. You can get your business off the ground and begin making serious cash.

Finally, if you enjoyed this book, please take the time to share your thoughts and post a review on Amazon. It'd be greatly appreciated!

Thank you and good luck!

Made in the USA
Monee, IL
03 December 2019